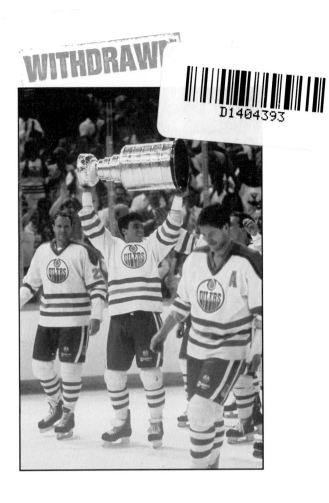

Grant Fuhr, the Oilers' all-star goalie.

OILERS

EDMONTON

BY ROSS RENNIE

CREATIVE EDUCATION INC.

Published by Creative Education, Inc.
123 S. Broad Street, Mankato, Minnesota 56001

Designed by Rita Marshall
Photos by Bruce Bennett Studios,
Frank Howard/Protography and Wide World Photos.

Library of Congress Cataloging-in-Publication Data

Rennie, Ross.
  The Edmonton Oilers/by Ross Rennie.
  p.   cm.
  Summary: Presents, in text and illustrations, the history of
the Edmonton Oilers hockey team, four-time Stanley Cup champions.
  ISBN 0-88682-278-5
  1. Edmonton Oilers (Hockey team)—History—Juvenile literature.
[1. Edmonton Oilers (Hockey team)—History.   2. Hockey—History.]
I. Title.
GV848.E36R46   1989
796.96'264'09712334—dc20   89-38494
                                                        CIP
                                                        AC

THE BEGINNINGS: 1973–1979

Edmonton is the largest and most populous city in the province of Alberta, as well as its capital. It is nestled within the rolling plains of the Parklands, considered to be one of the most abundant agricultural regions in Canada.

The city's beginnings date back to 1795, when Fort Edmonton was established on the North Saskatchewan River. It served as a fur trading post until 1798, when it was destroyed in an Indian attack. A new Fort Edmonton was constructed on the present site of the city in 1808.

Glenn Anderson is among the Oilers' career leaders in goals and assists.

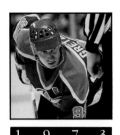

1 9 7 3

Before Gretzky and the NHL, Edmonton was selected as a franchise in the WHA.

The community functioned then, as now, as the main distribution point for goods en route to and from Alaska and northwestern Canada. From this comes Edmonton's nickname as the "Gateway to the North."

Despite the city's importance to agriculture and trade, it wasn't until oil was discovered nearby, in 1947, that Edmonton realized its potential. This strike established Canada as a large-scale oil producer and, at the same time, led to massive growth and expansion.

As an important regional center for thousands of hockey fans, it was only natural that Edmonton would be selected as the site for one of the twelve franchises of the World Hockey Association when it was founded in 1973. The WHA was an upstart league designed to challenge the National Hockey League for both major hockey talent and fan support. However, financial hardships ensued and it achieved only limited success. By the end of the 1970s, the league was ready to fold. As part of an agreement with the NHL, four WHA teams, including the Edmonton Oilers, joined the NHL prior to the 1979–80 season.

Most teams new to the league enjoyed only limited success during their first few years in the NHL, but the Oilers were hardly an ordinary expansion club. The story of the rise of the Edmonton Oilers from an expansion team to four-time Stanley Cup champions has one common thread: the emergence of Wayne Gretzky as the best player in the NHL. To understand how and why the Oilers have done so well in such a short time, it is important to learn about number 99 and how he became hockey's best player.

Wayne Gretzky helped Edmonton enjoy immediate success in the NHL.

The Oilers began their third year in the WHA and Gretzky turned sixteen.

Wayne Gretzky was born on January 26, 1961, in Brantford, Ontario, a city of seventy thousand with a rich hockey heritage. He was only two years old when he became fascinated by the game of hockey.

After seeing Wayne show an interest in the sport, his parents did everything possible to encourage him. Wayne's father, Walter, quickly bought his son ice skates. He also built a rink behind their house. At night he turned on the lawn sprinkler to create a personal ice arena for his son. Wayne was skating with a stick in his hands by the age of three. Under his father's watchful eye he practiced skating and stickhandling drills and learned how to play defensively.

It didn't take long for his remarkable playing skills to emerge. In 1971–72, eleven-year-old Gretzky scored 290 goals in his junior league. Wayne would regularly stuff five or six goals in the net while playing a complete game. His routine during this period was constant. Upon returning from school, he headed directly for his hockey equipment, laced on his skates, and played until dinnertime. After dinner he returned to his companions and resumed playing.

When Wayne was still eleven, he met his idol, Gordie Howe. The NHL's most durable superstar was clearly impressed. "God," said Howe, "he's got talent."

At age thirteen, in April 1974, Wayne had scored his thousandth career goal and already was suffering the emotional pains of a professional superstar. He was, quite simply, too good for his peers, and the parents of those children resented him. Yet Wayne remained polite and patient, a trait he has retained into adulthood.

"Since I was six years old," he explained, "I've had a lot of media attention. I was brought up that when people are interested in you, you have a responsibility to them, that you have to watch what you say and do whenever you're in the public eye."

When he was sixteen, Gretzky was drafted by the Sault Ste. Marie Greyhounds. Gretzky had hoped to obtain uniform number 9, the same as he had in Brantford and the same worn by his idol, Gordie Howe, but it was already spoken for so he picked number 99. The Ontario Major League was as tough as its reputation, but Wayne was up to the challenge.

At the age of seventeen, Wayne Gretzky turned professional.

Wherever Gretzky played, the results were at the very least superlative. In Montreal he participated in the World Junior championships and paced the pack with eight goals and 17 points in six games. He broke the Greyhounds' scoring record with 70 goals and 182 points and excelled in virtually every department. He was voted the rookie of the year and was presented with the William Hanley Trophy for quality and gentlemanly play.

In June 1978, when Wayne Gretzky was seventeen years old, he was signed by the Indianapolis Racers of the WHA. The signing upset many NHL executives, who felt it was a bad idea to bring such young players into professional hockey.

"I know I will have to go out and prove myself again," said Gretzky at the time. "The challenge is there."

Gretzky is hockey's most prolific scorer of all-time. (pages 10–11)

Gretzky soon showed that he was more than equal to the task. However, he was not destined to play for Indianapolis for long. After only a few games with the Racers, he was traded to the Edmonton Oilers, who were playing their last year in the WHA.

His new coach was Glen Sather, an average NHL player who had developed patience, insight, and an understanding of the average athlete, qualities that made him a superior leader and coach.

As talented as Gretzky was, Sather saw room for improvement in his young star. The observant coach helped Wayne overcome his defensive weaknesses.

During a match with the Cincinnati Stingers, Gretzky made a defensive mistake which provided Cincinnati with the puck and a goal. Gretzky returned to the bench and waited for his next shift. It didn't come.

When it finally did come, Gretzky responded. He scored three goals to help the Oilers overcome a 2–1 deficit and win 5–2.

"That," said Sather, "was the turning point in his career. He could have pouted and sulked. Not just anyone could keep the motivation with a contract like his. But he wants to be the best."

Under Sather's guidance, Gretzky flourished. By the end of his first season, Wayne had scored 110 points and was named the WHA's rookie of the year.

1 9 8 0

Coach Glen Sather led the Oilers to twenty-eight victories in their first NHL season.

When the Oilers joined the NHL the following year, the question was, once again, whether or not Gretzky would be able to keep up his outstanding performance at this higher level of play. By the end of the season, all doubt was erased as Wayne had tied Marcel Dionne for the NHL scoring lead with 137 points and the Oilers had squeezed into the final play-off spot. Gretzky also was awarded the Lady Byng Trophy as the NHL's most gentlemanly player and was presented the Hart Trophy as the league's most valuable player.

Even though the Oilers were eliminated in the first round of the play-offs, Gretzky and his teammates had served notice to the rest of the NHL that they were a club to be reckoned with. Their performance that year foreshadowed the club's meteoric rise from an expansion team to the league's premier club. During the 1980s, the Edmonton team never failed to qualify for the play-offs, going to the finals five times. The Oilers won Lord Stanley's Cup four times within a span of five seasons to reign as the undisputed champions of the NHL.

The prime factor behind the ascent of the Oilers was, of course, the unparalleled play of Wayne Gretzky, or the

"Great One," as he was soon known throughout hockey. "He's the premier attraction in the National Hockey League," Sather said. "He's the most exciting young player in the league."

Sather was not alone in his assessment of Gretzky. Even his opponents couldn't help but watch him in amazement. "There are times," said former Winnipeg Jets defenseman Dave Babych, "when you sit on the bench and you almost want to clap your hands at some of the things he does."

During his second year in the league, Gretzky played in every one of the Oilers' 80 games and totaled 55 goals, a record breaking 109 assists, and a record breaking 164 points. He was only twenty years old.

Gretzky's point total catapulted him far above the previous mark held by Phil Esposito (152). Furthermore, his 109 assists smashed the record of another ice immortal, Bobby Orr, who had produced 102 assists in 1970.

Coach Glen Sather could not say enough about his star. "Remember," said Sather. "Wayne doesn't have an Orr passing him the puck like Espo did. A guy like Wayne should be a national treasure. There's no limit to what he can do."

He also helped Edmonton to finish in the fourteenth spot and qualify for the play-offs. The Oilers lost only one of their last twelve games and three of their final seventeen.

In the postseason, the Oilers were due to face the tough Montreal Canadiens, who were led by their star, Guy Lafleur. Most critics hardly gave the Oilers a chance. After all, they had finished twenty-nine points behind Montreal and there was no reason to think the Canadiens would not sweep the Oilers.

Paul Coffey joined Gretzky and the Oilers for the 1980–81 season.

1 9 8 2

The Oilers won their first Smythe Division championship by recording 111 points.

In talent, there seemed to be little comparison—apart from Gretzky. The Canadiens had players with high skill levels and years of experience. Defensemen Serge Savard and Guy Lapointe had played for many Stanley Cup winners and besides Lafleur they had forwards such as Steve Shutt, Rejean Houle, Mark Napier and Yvon Lambert who were all artists on the ice. But even though the Oilers were the underdogs in the series, they were ready to show the rest of the league that their club could mount a challenge for the Cup.

The series opened on April 8, 1981, at the Forum in Montreal. The Oilers had appeared twice in Montreal during the regular season and had scored only one goal.

Paul Coffey was instrumental in the Oilers' victory over Montreal.

To the amazement of many, the Oilers swept the series in three fast games. Thus, Edmonton advanced to the next round of the play-offs, where they faced the New York Islanders, the defending Stanley Cup champions.

Although the Islanders prevailed in the series, New York was quick to admit that the Oilers had given them a scare.

"It was more than a classic Stanley Cup series," said Denis Potvin. "It was a series based almost entirely on emotion. It was tough to play them. They were all over the ice. They made it so frustrating for us."

The Oilers were unruffled by their defeat. "There are a lot of teams that are not in the play-offs for a couple of years and they're going to be the same way next year," coach Sather commented. "We know where we are headed. Some teams don't. Our management isn't panicking. We feel like we are the Islanders of 1972 or 1973, that our time is going to come all at once."

As the 1981–82 season began, the Oilers were playing winning hockey and Gretzky was scoring at a fast pace. By the time he had reached game thirty-eight, he had accumulated forty-five goals. The mark of fifty goals in fifty games that had been set by Maurice "the Rocket" Richard in the 1944–45 season and equaled by Mike Bossy in the previous season was in danger.

In game thirty-nine against the Philadelphia Flyers on December 30, 1981, Wayne scored five goals to reach the fifty-goal mark. Immediately following the game, Gretzky phoned his parents from the dressing room. "I got more satisfaction out of the call than out of the record," said

1 9 8 2

After only his first year, Grant Fuhr was named to the NHL's Second All-Star team.

Glenn Anderson scored over one hundred points during the 1981–82 season. (pages 18–19)

Walter Gretzky. "I guess it was just a matter of time but I never in my wildest imagination thought he'd do it in 39 games."

Gretzky went on to have the greatest offensive season in the history of the sport. He completed the eighty-game schedule with 92 goals and 120 assists, for 212 points. He had broken all the records and had guided his team to the second best record in the NHL.

The amazing development of Gretzky was the most important reason for the Oilers to think they would have a bright future. In a space of four years, he had won three scoring titles and tied for a fourth. He won numerous other awards as well. But the individual awards paled next to the one Gretzky truly longed for. When asked to name the three greatest ambitions he still had in hockey, his reply was, "First to win the Stanley Cup. Second to win the Stanley Cup. Third to win the Stanley Cup!"

THE GLORY YEARS: 1983–1988

1 9 8 4

The Oilers defeated the New York Islanders for their first Stanley Cup championship.

In 1983–84 Gretzky and his club set out in earnest to win professional hockey's most cherished award. After qualifying for the play-offs with ease, the Oilers eliminated Winnipeg, Calgary, and Minnesota before meeting the New York Islanders in the championship series. Edmonton had lost to the Islanders in the Stanley Cup finals just one year before.

Game one at Nassau Coliseum was a classic defensive battle that saw the Oilers prevail 1–0 on a goal at 1:55 of the third period by Kevin McClelland. The tough center scored on a perfect pass from Pat Hughes after Islander right wing Duane Sutter had coughed up the puck in his own end of the ice.

The win ended a ten-game losing streak that the Oilers had against the Islanders. This victory, along with the experience gained by Edmonton in the previous year, enabled the Oilers to go on to defeat the Islanders four games to one. The Edmonton Oilers were Stanley Cup champions.

"They worked hard in every shift, in every game," said Islander left wing Bob Bourne. "They wanted it so bad; they really sacrificed in this series."

Not only did the Oilers win the Cup, but they also collected a number of major awards. Wayne Gretzky won his

Esa Tikkanen made his debut with the Oilers during the 1985 play-offs.

fifth consecutive Hart Trophy as the most valuable player of the league. He also won the Art Ross trophy for winning his fourth straight scoring title.

But Gretzky did not win the championship by himself. Other stars were emerging on the Oilers' squad. Left wing Mark Messier stepped out of Gretzky's shadow by delivering a sparkling performance to earn the Conn Smythe trophy as the play-off's most valuable player. A native of Edmonton, Messier was the son of a former coach of the Oiler's farm club in Moncton, New Brunswick. Equally proficient at shooting, passing, and defense, Mark was selected to three All-Star teams during the 1980s. He also ranks as the Oilers' third all-time scoring leader.

Regarded as one of the top players in the game, Messier always gave his best effort on the ice. "You're only as good as your last shift," he said. "You must prove yourself game after game."

Paul Coffey was another Oiler who was beginning to make a name for himself throughout the league. The defenseman finished the season as runner-up to Gretzky for the Ross Trophy. Coffey continued his stellar play throughout the decade. He was named to the NHL All-Star team five consecutive seasons during the mid-1980s and twice was awarded the Norris Trophy as the league's best defenseman.

Another key player was Jari Kurri; on the way to the Oilers' championship Kurri established a league scoring record for right wings, becoming only the third player in the history of the league to score seventy or more goals in a single season. He also was awarded the Lady Byng Award for the league's most gentlemanly player.

1 9 8 5

Paul Coffey won the James Norris Trophy, given to the NHL's most outstanding defenseman.

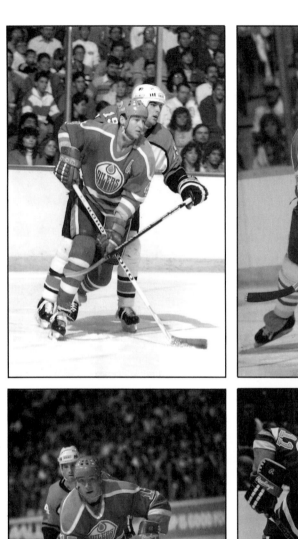

(clockwise): Kevin Lowe, Craig Simpson, Mark Messier, Jari Kurri.

Having won two consecutive Cups in 1983–84 and 1984–85, the Oilers took dead aim on their third championship as the next season approached. Led by the Great Gretzky, they easily overpowered all Smythe Division opposition in the early months of the season. Sather had infused fresh blood into the club with the additions of Messier, Coffey, and Kurri. Only five players remained from the team's first year in the NHL: Wayne Gretzky, Dave Hunter, Dave Lumley, Dave Semenko, and Lee Fogolin.

1 9 8 7

Jari Kurri was named to the NHL's First Team All-Star squad.

The Oilers finished the season high atop the Smythe Division with a 56-17-7 record for 119 points. They were the first team to win the NHL's new President's Trophy, which goes to the club with the most points over the regular season. Edmonton knew they had a real chance to win a third consecutive championship. This would firmly establish the Oilers as one of the greatest teams of all-time. But their hopes were dashed when the club lost in the division finals to a tough Calgary Flames team.

Not to be deterred by this setback, the Oilers again set out to prove themselves. They succeeded by winning two more back-to-back championships in 1986–87 and 1987–88. Once again, the club was led by the splendid play of Messier, Kurri, and, of course, the incomparable Gretzky. Despite the loss of Paul Coffey in a trade to Pittsburgh prior to the 1987–88 season, the Oilers seemed to lose little momentum.

A large degree of their success can also be attributed to the fine goaltending of Grant Fuhr, considered by many to be the finest goalie in the league. Fuhr, who had the highest winning percentage in the NHL, was awarded the

Grant Fuhr, one of the NHL's premier goaltenders. (pages 26–27)

25

Steve Smith (right) provided Grant Fuhr with steady support on defense.

Vezina Trophy in 1987–88 as the NHL's best goaltender. That year he ranked first in the league among goalies in games, minutes played, and wins.

Fuhr's splendid play was not overlooked by his teammates. "You can be in a 6-6 hockey game, but what counts is the guy who makes the big save to keep that seventh goal from going in—and Grant always did that." commented Wayne Gretzky. "He was relentless."

The pressure of tending goal in the Stanley Cup finals did not seem to affect Fuhr. "I like what I do," Grant said. "I enjoy what I do, so it doesn't bother me as much. There's always the fear of losing, but we've been lucky, we haven't lost too much."

"When he gets behind the mask, nothing seems to bother him," said Glen Sather. Fuhr—who played golf during the play-offs to relax—proved the truth of his coach's words by making spectacular saves game after game, year after year.

TODAY'S EDMONTON OILERS: 1988 AND BEYOND

Having won four NHL championships in the span of five seasons left Edmonton on the top of the world. It didn't seem that anything could stop this team. But on August 9, 1988, everything would change.

Jimmy Carson was obtained from the Los Angeles Kings in the Wayne Gretzky trade.

On this day the Oilers traded the immortal Wayne Gretzky, along with Mike Krushelnyski and Marty Mc-Sorley, to the Los Angeles Kings. In return they received players Jimmy Carson, Martin Gelinas, three first-round draft picks, and $15 million in cash.

The lament over Gretzky's departure was heard not only in Edmonton, but throughout the nation. Many Canadians, who considered Gretzky a national treasure, were stunned by the announcement. They could not believe Wayne could leave his native land to play hockey in southern California.

It was clear that the Oilers would never be the same. Gretzky had been the club's all-time leader in games played, goals, assists, and total points. He had been named to the All-Star team in each of his nine seasons in the NHL. For many fans, Gretzky *was* the Edmonton Oilers.

To lose such a franchise player can be devastating to a team. As the 1988–89 season unfolded, it was clear the Oilers weren't the overpowering team they had been in the past. But their maturity and talent shone through and carried them to the seventh best record in hockey.

But Edmonton's real test came in the play-offs where they came up against their famous former teammate as

Jimmy Carson has the ability to be a perennial all-star.

Jari Kurri continues to be one of the NHL's finest.

1 9 9 0

*Grant Fuhr hopes to
lead the Oilers to
another Stanley Cup
championship.*

they faced the Kings in the first round. After the Oilers built a three-to-one game lead, Gretzky and his teammates charged back to win the series. It was the first time in six years that the Oilers did not advance past the first round of the play-offs.

The Oilers have enjoyed a phenomenal amount of success in the short time they have been in the NHL. Under Sather's guidance, and with the help of the "Great Gretzky," the Oilers were able to establish a dynasty in their first decade in the league.

While the present era of Edmonton's dominance in the NHL may have passed, the future is still bright for the club. Anchored by Messier, Kurri, and Fuhr, and with such rising young stars as Craig Simpson and Jimmy Carson, the Oilers are sure to be serious contenders for Lord Stanley's Cup in the years to come.

DATE DUE		
27 '9		
13 '9		
'92		
'9		